Carving Early American Weathervanes

16 Decorative Projects

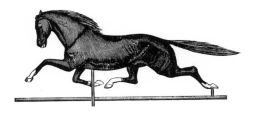

by

Anthony Hillman

Dover Publications, Inc.

New York

To
Ted and Jane Von Bosse

Note: The instructions appear at the *back*
of the book, following the patterns.

Published in Canada by General Publishing Company, Ltd.,
30 Lesmill Road, Don Mills, Toronto, Ontario.
Published in the United Kingdom by Constable and Company, Ltd.

Carving Early American Weathervanes is a new work,
first published by Dover Publications, Inc., in 1986.
These patterns and drawings are not to be used for
printed reproduction without permission.

Manufactured in the United States of America
Dover Publications, Inc., 31 East 2nd Street,
Mineola, N.Y. 11501

Library of Congress Cataloging-in-Publication Data

Hillman, Anthony.
Carving early American weathervanes.

1. Wood-carving—Patterns. 2. Vanes. I. Title.
TT199.7.H54 1986   736'.4   86-8933
ISBN 0-486-25223-X

"DEXTER"
(1865)

Minimum Thickness of Wood at This Scale: ¾"

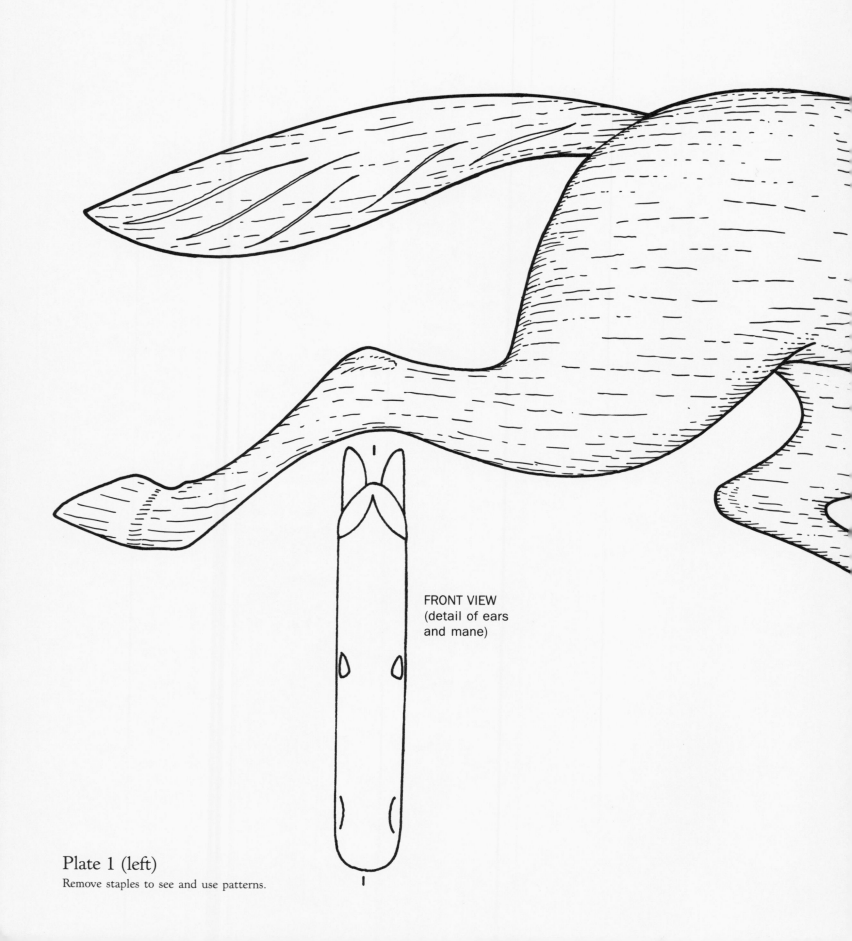

FRONT VIEW
(detail of ears
and mane)

Plate 1 (left)

Remove staples to see and use patterns.

CODFISH
(1760)

Minimum Thickness of Wood at This Scale: ¾″

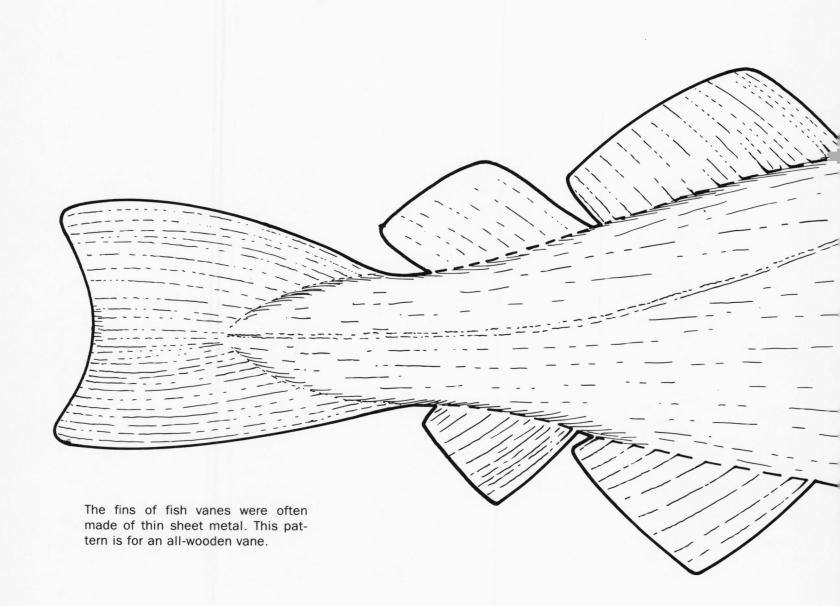

The fins of fish vanes were often made of thin sheet metal. This pattern is for an all-wooden vane.

Plate 2 (left)

Remove staples to see and use patterns.

SEAHORSE
(1860)

Minimum Thickness of Wood at This Scale: ¾″

Plate 3 (left)

Remove staples to see and use patterns.

WEATHERCOCK
(1700)

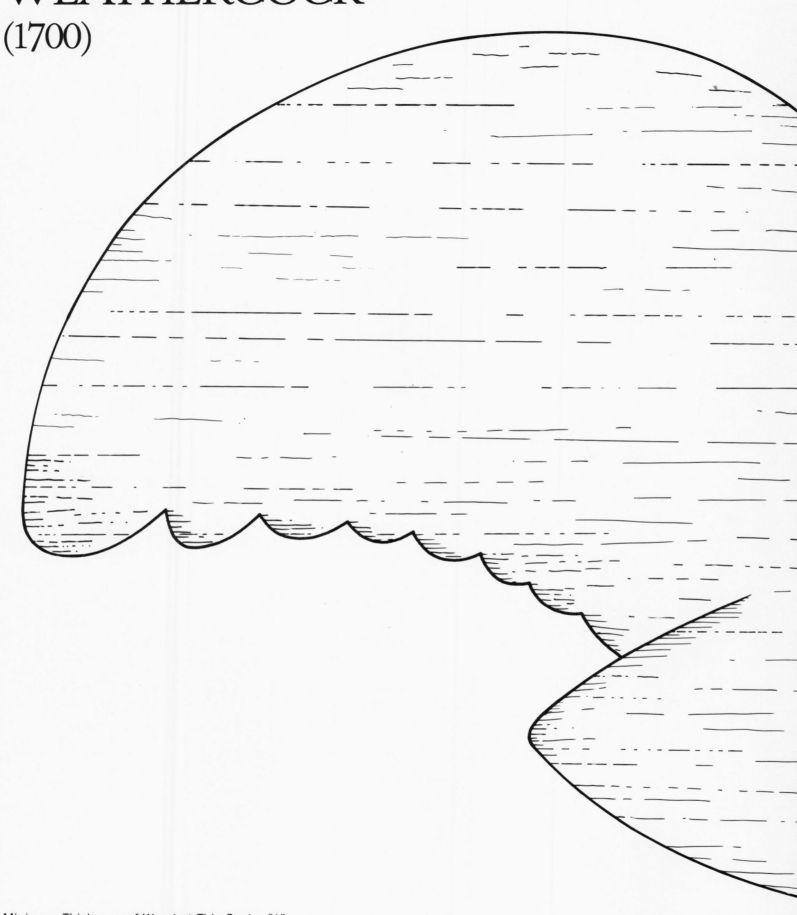

Minimum Thickness of Wood at This Scale: ¾″

Plate 4 (left)
Remove staples to see and use patterns.

SPERM WHALE
(1780)

Minimum Thickness of Wood at This Scale: ¾"

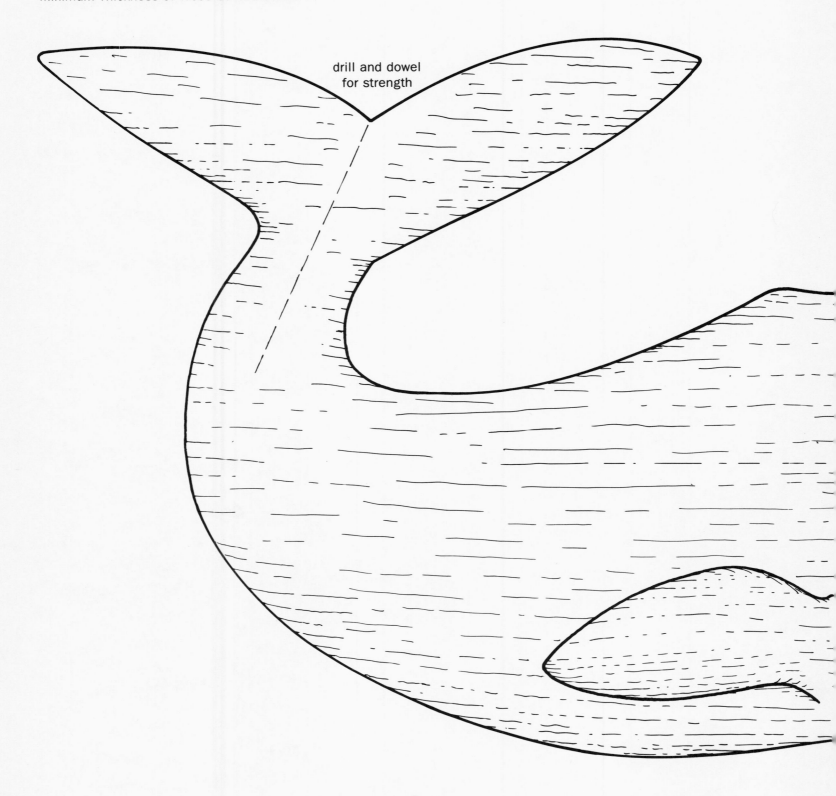

drill and dowel
for strength

Plate 5 (left)
Remove staples to see and use patterns.

RIGHT WHALE
(Baleen Whale)

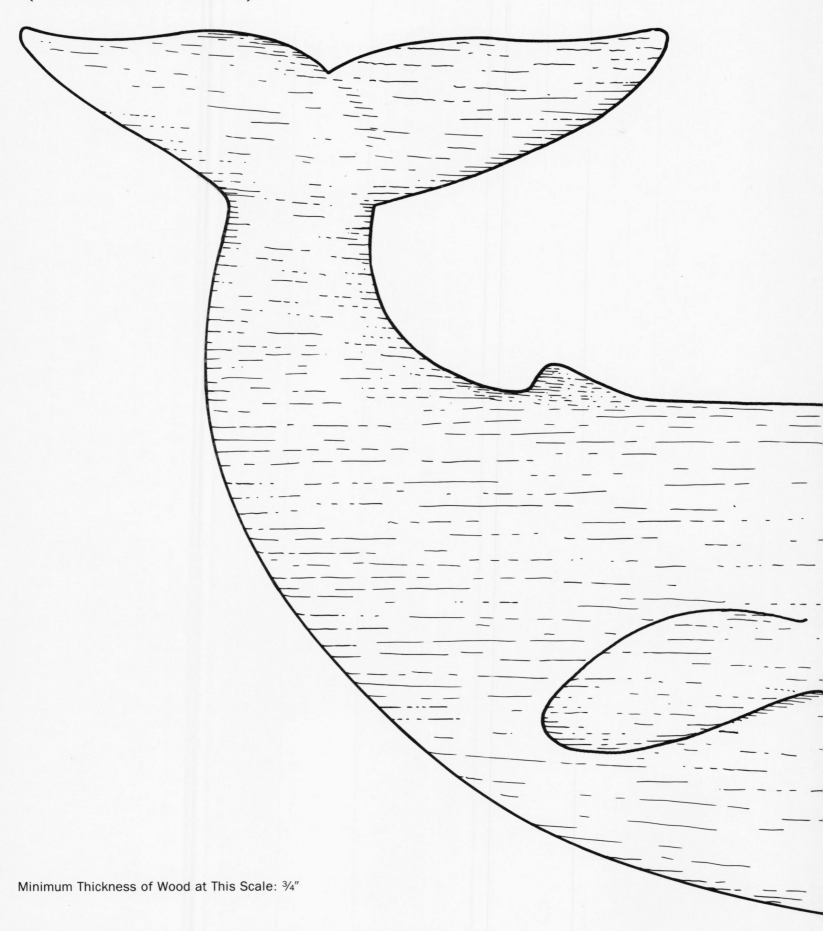

Minimum Thickness of Wood at This Scale: ¾"

Plate 6 (left)
Remove staples to see and use patterns.

JUMPING DEER
(1880)

Minimum Thickness of Wood at This Scale: ¾"

Antlers: 0.025" sheet copper or tin at this scale

Plate 7 (left)

Remove staples to see and use patterns.

EAGLE
(Bald Eagle)

Minimum Thickness of Wood at This Scale: ½"

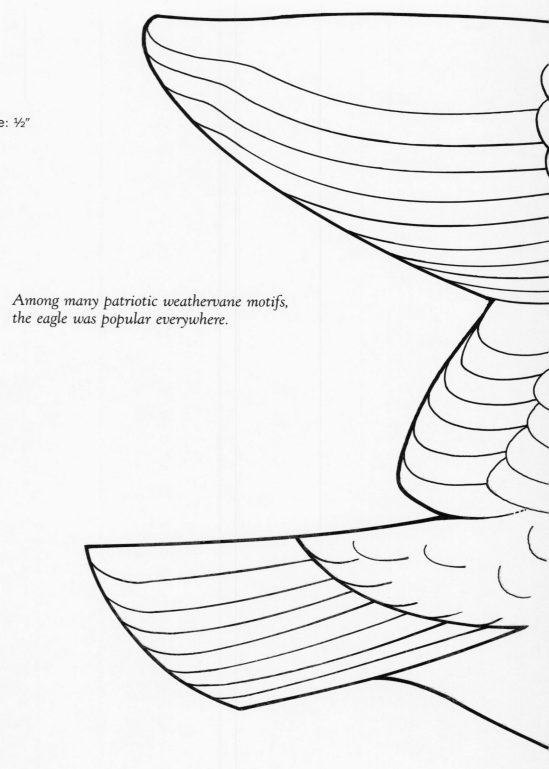

Among many patriotic weathervane motifs,
the eagle was popular everywhere.

Plate 8 (left)

Remove staples to see and use patterns.

SWORDFISH
(1910)

Minimum Thickness of Wood at This Scale: ¾″

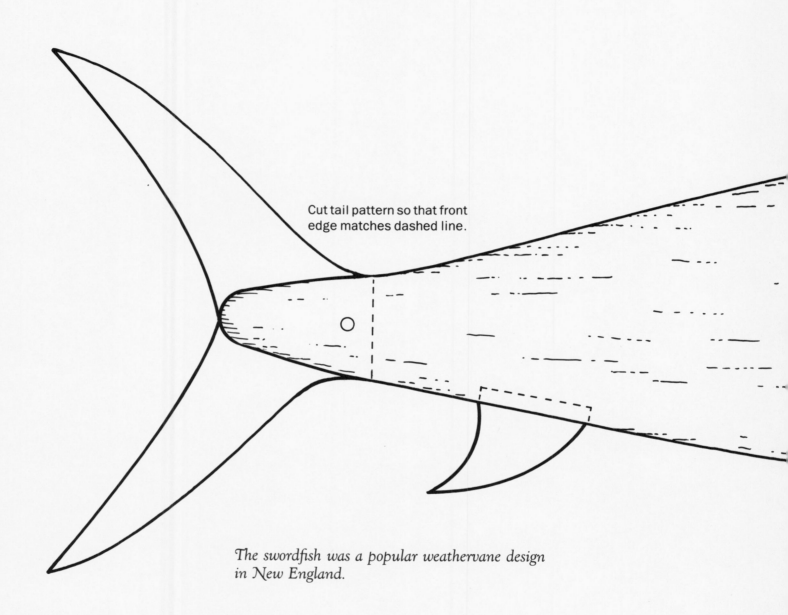

Cut tail pattern so that front
edge matches dashed line.

*The swordfish was a popular weathervane design
in New England.*

Plate 9 (left)
Remove staples to see and use patterns.

FLYING GOOSE
(Canada Goose)

Minimum Thickness of Wood at This Scale: ½″

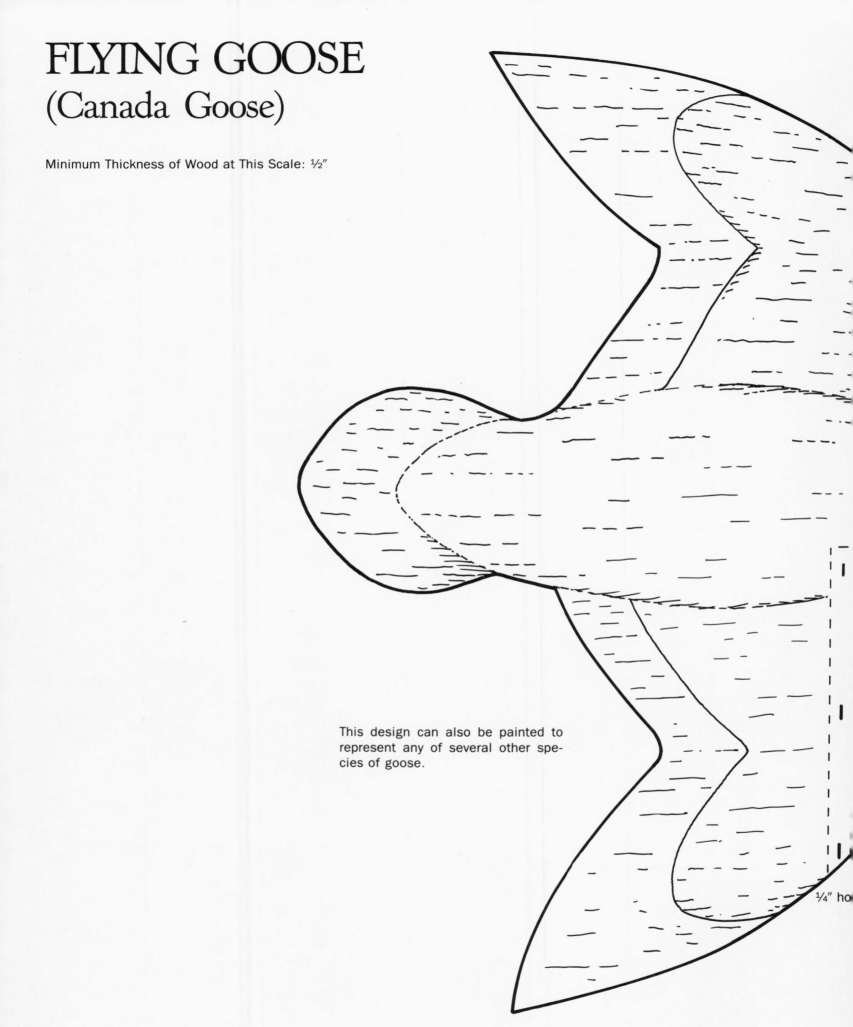

This design can also be painted to represent any of several other species of goose.

¼″ ho

Plate 10 (left)
Remove staples to see and use patterns.

MERINO RAM

Minimum Thickness of Wood at This Scale: ¾"

Plate 11 (left)

Remove staples to see and use patterns.

Baseboard: 15" long × ¾" wide × ⅜" thick
Screw or nail to three rear legs.

COW

Minimum Thickness of Wood at This Scale: ¾″

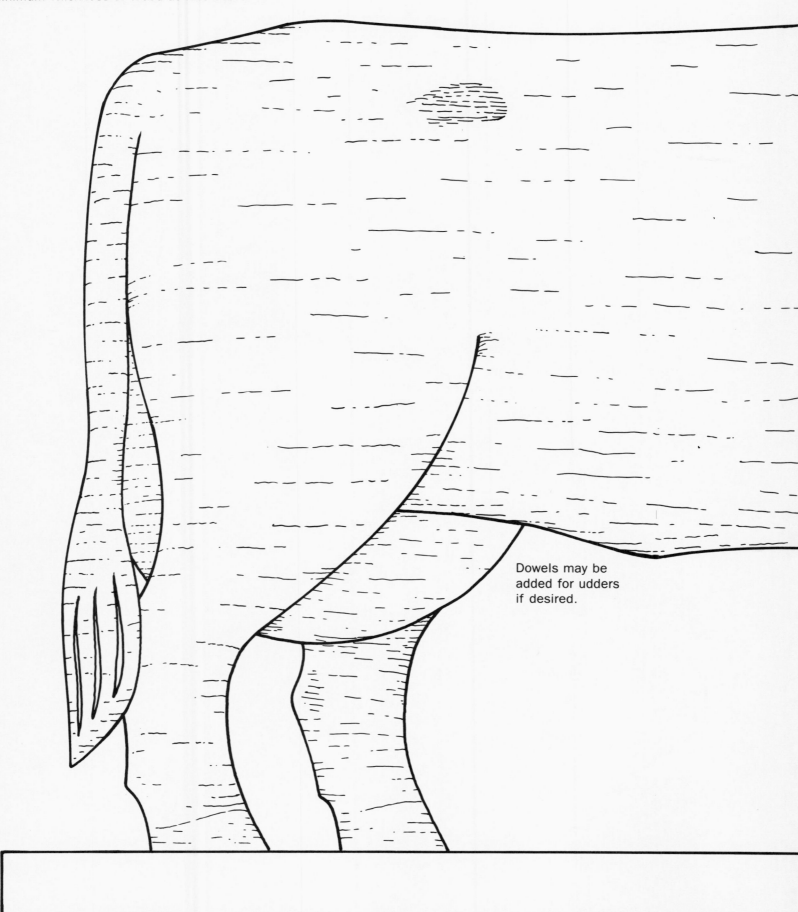

Dowels may be
added for udders
if desired.

Plate 12 (left)

Baseboard: 15¼″ long × ¾″ wide × ¾″ thick

Remove staples to see and use patterns.

PIG

Tail made from
copper nail
or heavy wire.

Minimum Thickness of Wood at This Scale: ¾"

Baseboard: 15" long × ¾" wide × ¾" thick

Plate 13 (left)
Remove staples to see and use patterns.

STANDING HORSE

Minimum Thickness of Wood at This Scale: 1″

Plate 14 (left)

Remove staples to see and use patterns.

Baseboard: 12½″ long × 1″ wide × ¾″ thick
Attach baseboard to three rear legs using nails or screws.

DOVE & TULIP
(Ohio, 1835)

Minimum Thickness of Wood at This Scale: ⅜"

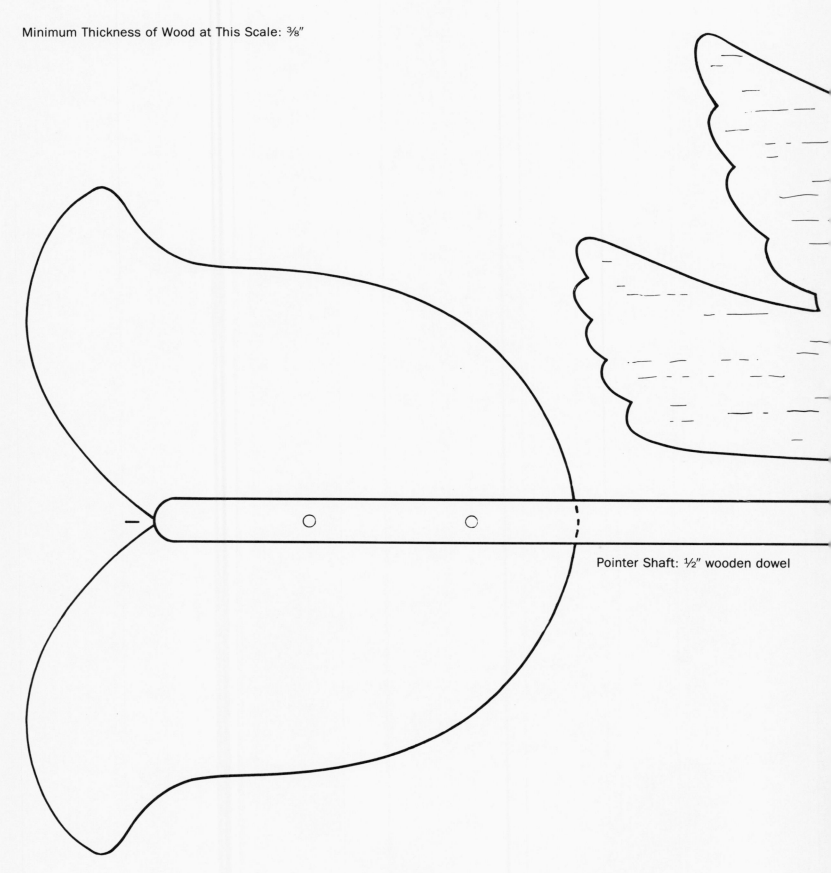

Pointer Shaft: ½" wooden dowel

Plate 15 (left)

Remove staples to see and use patterns.

POINTER

Minimum Thickness of Wood at This Scale: ¾″

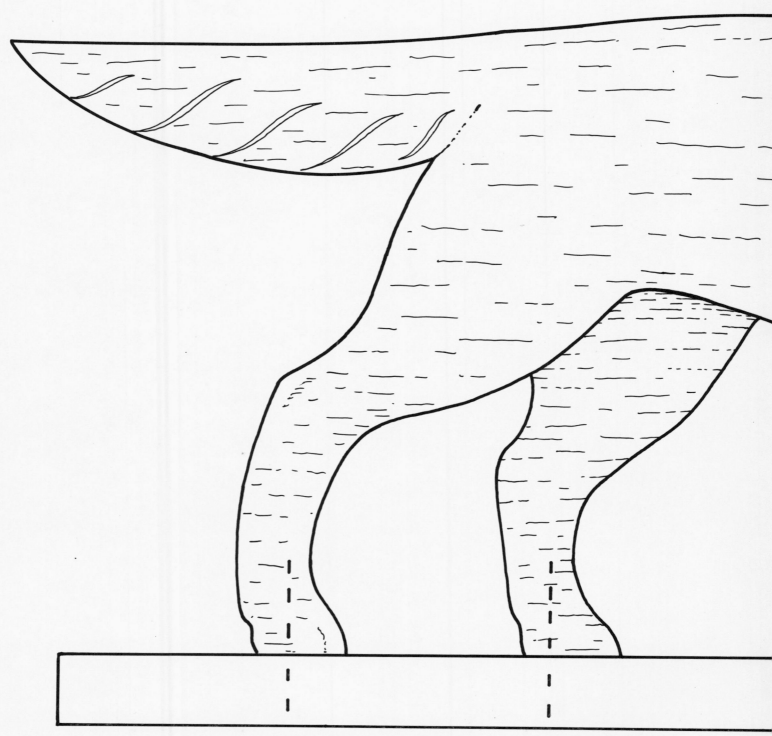

Baseboard: 14½″ long × ¾″ wide × ¾″ thick
Use screws or nails to fasten hind legs to baseboard.

Plate 16 (left)

Remove staples to see and use patterns.

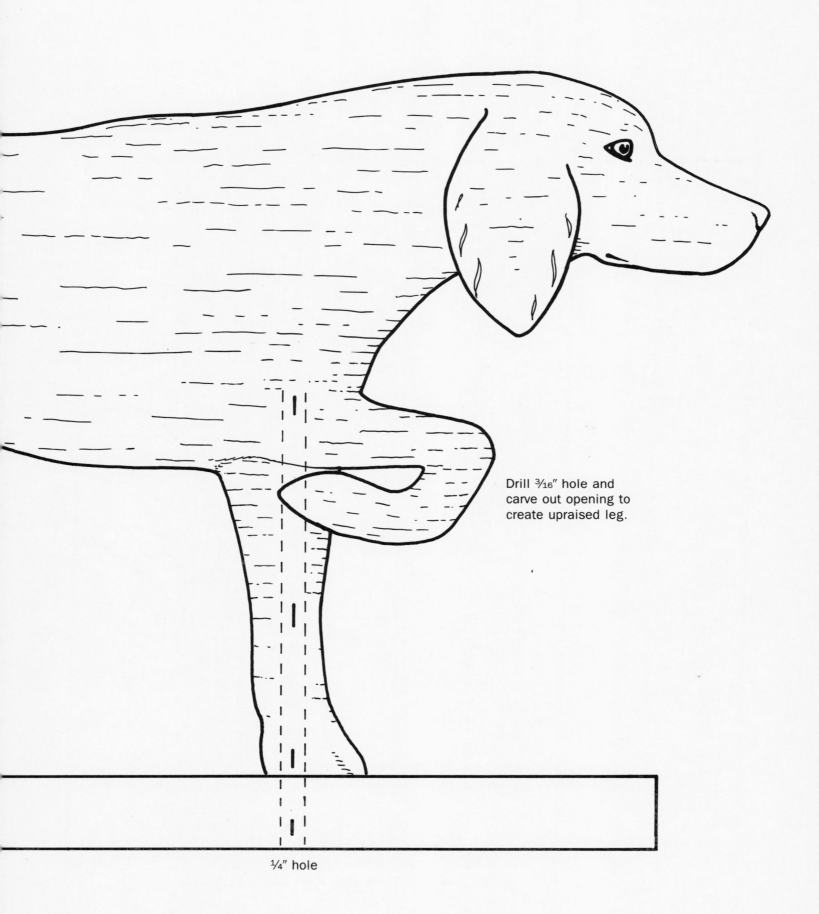

Drill ³⁄₁₆″ hole and
carve out opening to
create upraised leg.

¼″ hole

Plate 16 (right)
Remove staples to see and use patterns.

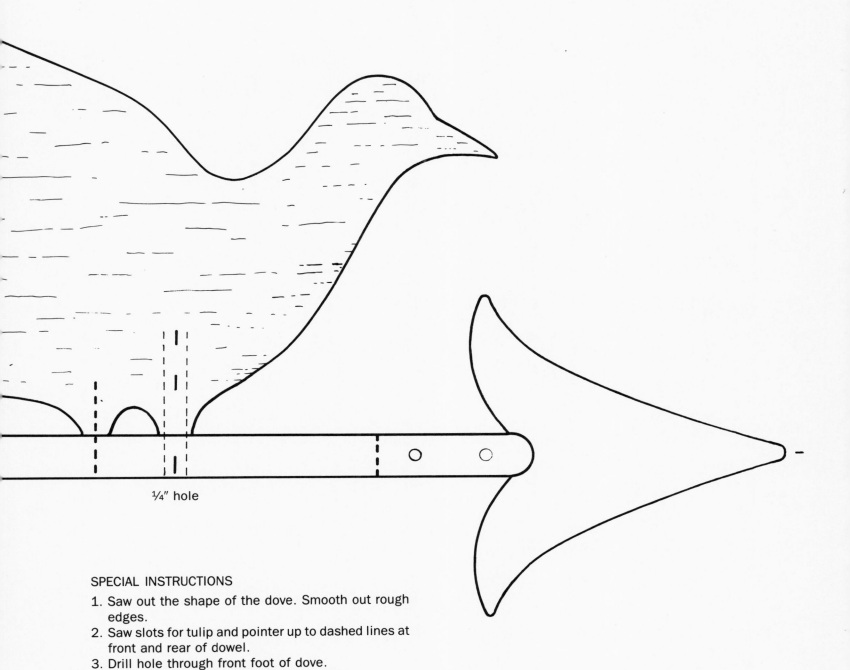

¼" hole

SPECIAL INSTRUCTIONS

1. Saw out the shape of the dove. Smooth out rough edges.
2. Saw slots for tulip and pointer up to dashed lines at front and rear of dowel.
3. Drill hole through front foot of dove.
4. Drill corresponding hole through dowel.
5. Insert length of metal tubing into hole in dowel shaft and dove, joining the two.
6. Use nail or screw through rear foot of dove to secure dove to shaft.
7. Cut tulip and pointer from sheet copper. Insert in slots, drill holes where shown, and secure with copper brads.

Plate 15 (right)

¼" hole

Plate 14 (right)
Remove staples to see and use patterns.

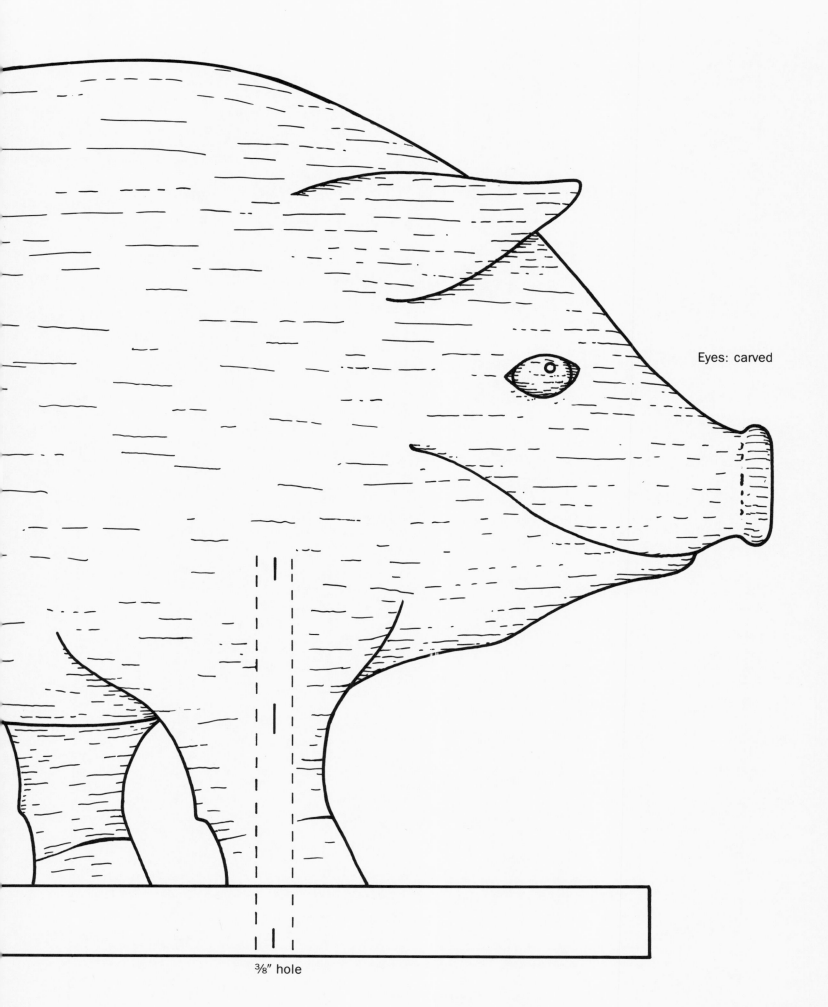

Eyes: carved

⅜" hole

Plate 13 (right)

Remove staples to see and use patterns.

³⁄₈" hole

Plate 12 (right)
Remove staples to see and use patterns.

⅜″ hole

Plate 11 (right)

Remove staples to see and use patterns.

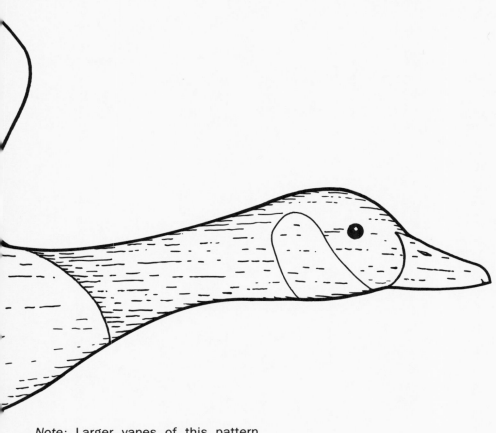

Note: Larger vanes of this pattern should be reinforced at the junction of the lower wing and the body, where the hole for the mount passes through.

Plate 10 (right)

Remove staples to see and use patterns.

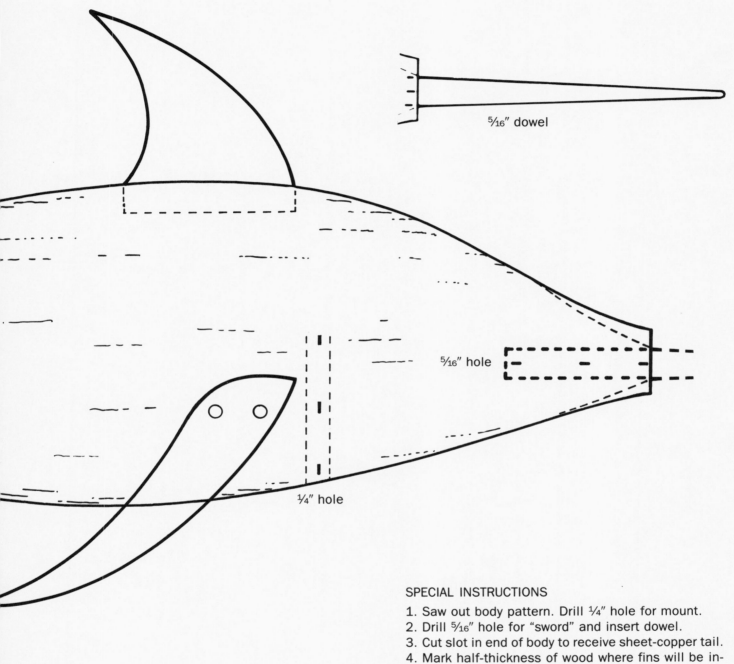

5/16" dowel

5/16" hole

1/4" hole

SPECIAL INSTRUCTIONS

1. Saw out body pattern. Drill 1/4" hole for mount.
2. Drill 5/16" hole for "sword" and insert dowel.
3. Cut slot in end of body to receive sheet-copper tail.
4. Mark half-thickness of wood where fins will be inserted. Round off edges of body.
5. Carve body so it flows smoothly into sword (as shown by dashed lines). Taper sword.
6. Cut out fins of sheet copper. Cut slots into body for top and bottom fins where shown, and insert fins. The side fins are nailed on (or you may use copper-plated brads as I did). Also use a nail or brad to secure the tail fin in its slot.

Plate 9 (right)

Eyes: 6mm yellow glass,
or ¼" carved

¼" hole

Plate 8 (right)
Remove staples to see and use patterns.

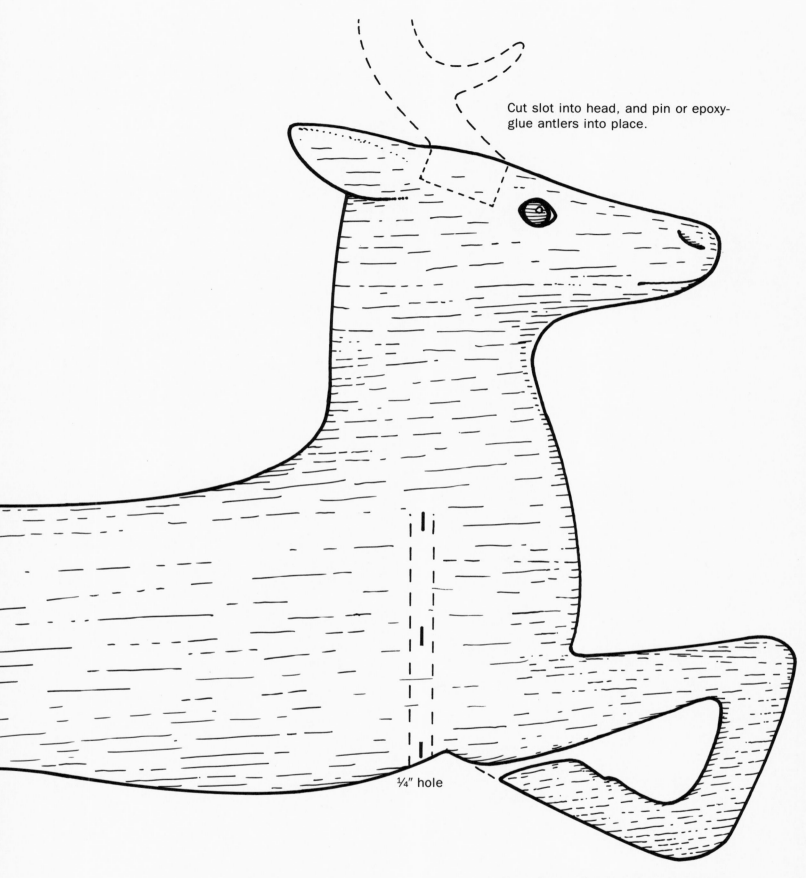

Cut slot into head, and pin or epoxy-glue antlers into place.

¼″ hole

Note: Saw at first only around *outside* of leg pattern. When carving is nearly complete, saw inside bend of leg, and carve to finish.

Plate 7 (right)

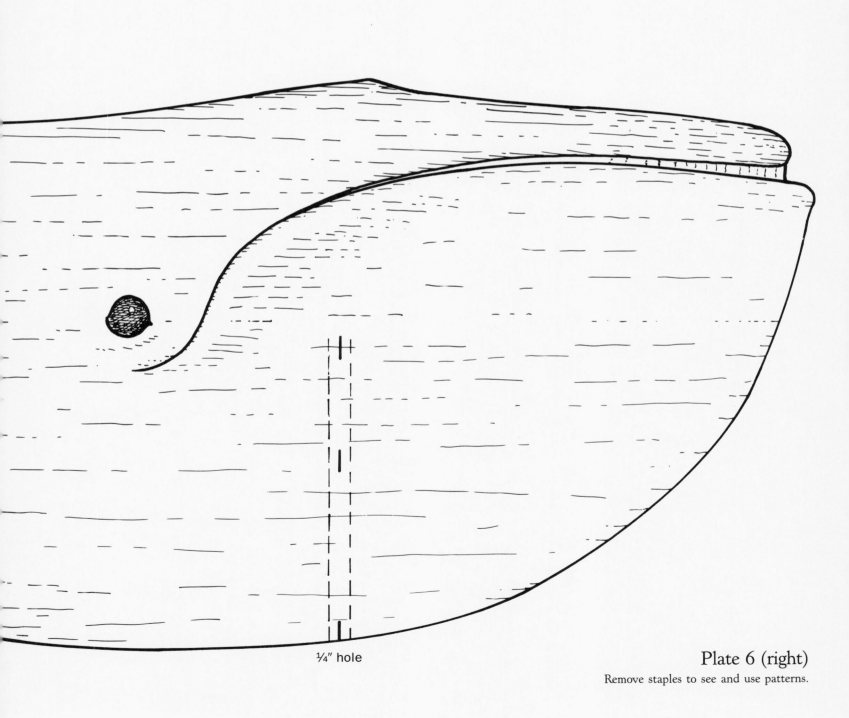

¼″ hole

Plate 6 (right)

Remove staples to see and use patterns.

The abundance of whale vanes in New England reflected the importance of this sea mammal to New Englanders. Even today the whale remains one of the most popular weathervane motifs.

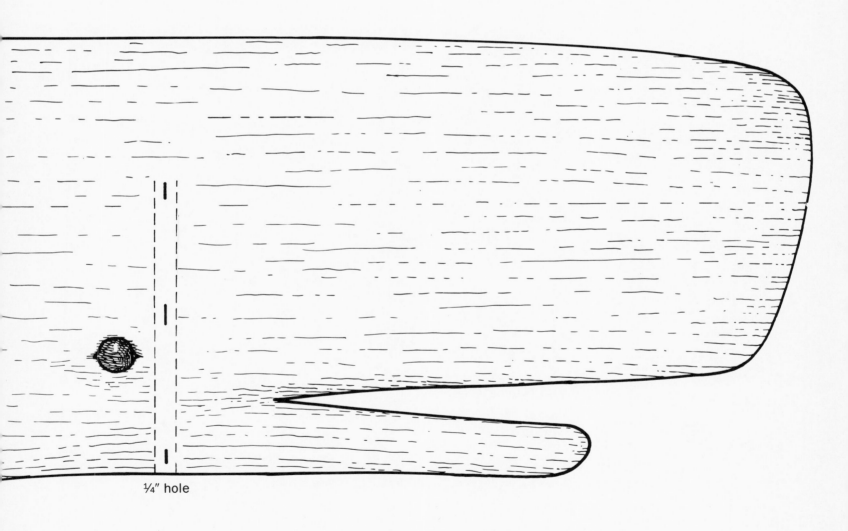

¼" hole

Plate 5 (right)
Remove staples to see and use patterns.

Applied leather may be used for the comb if desired.

¼" hole

Plate 4 (right)

Remove staples to see and use patterns.

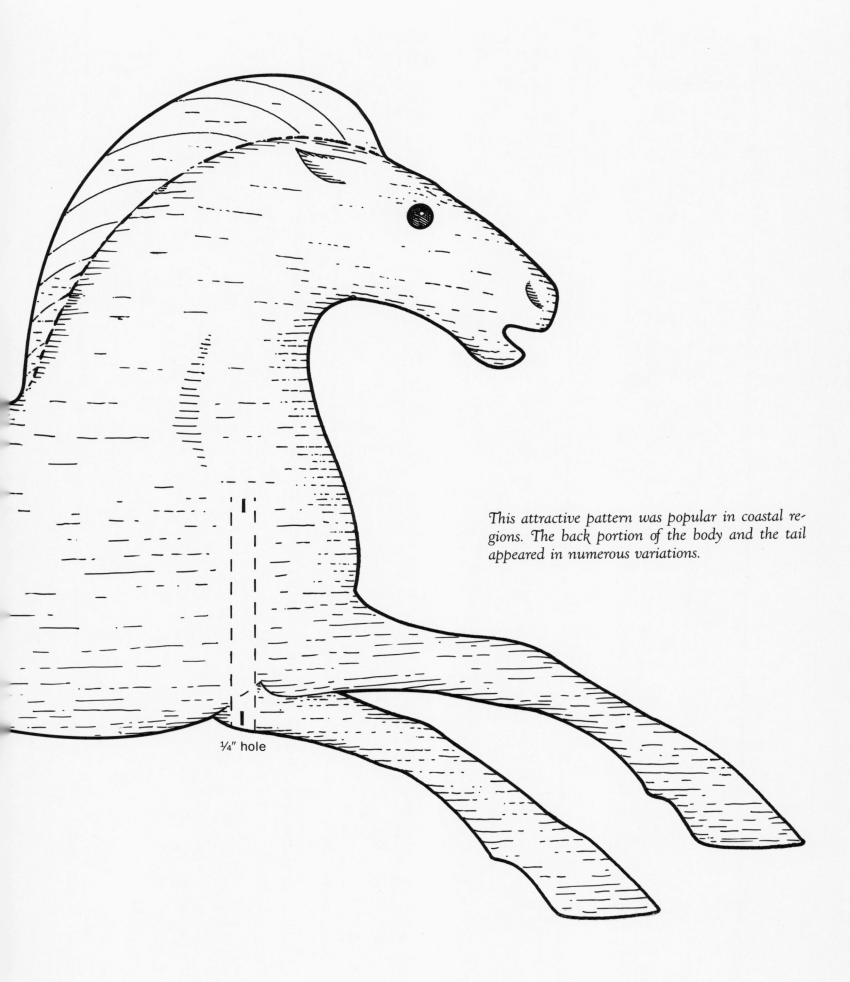

This attractive pattern was popular in coastal regions. The back portion of the body and the tail appeared in numerous variations.

¼" hole

Plate 3 (right)

Remove staples to see and use patterns.

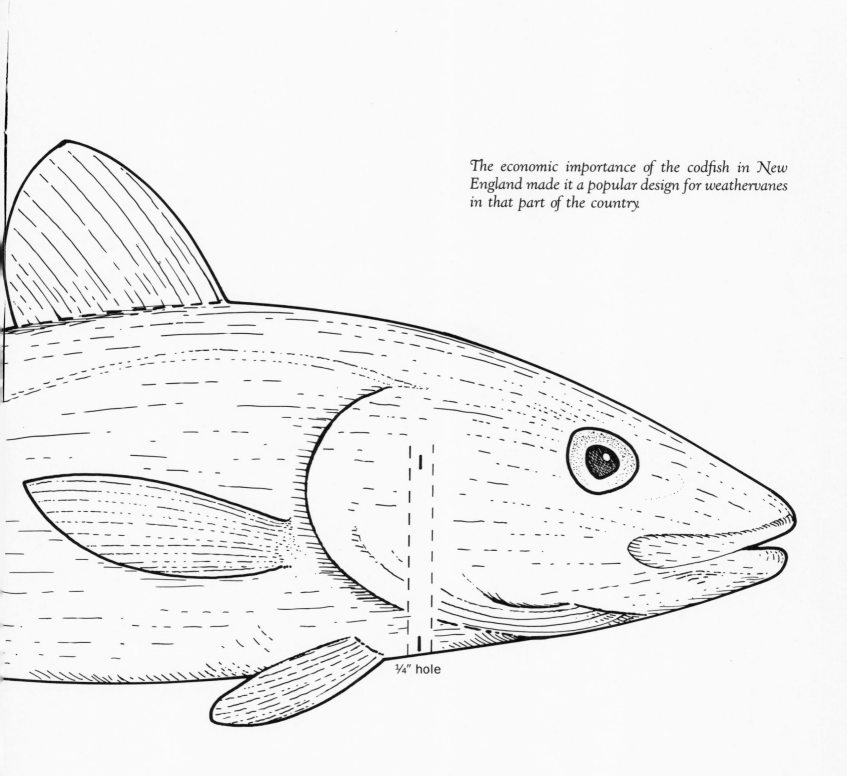

The economic importance of the codfish in New
England made it a popular design for weathervanes
in that part of the country.

¼" hole

Plate 2 (right)
Remove staples to see and use patterns.

¼" hole

This profile of Dexter, a famous trotter featured in a Currier & Ives lithograph, was popular with nineteenth-century weathervane makers.

Plate 1 (right)
Remove staples to see and use patterns.

How to Carve
Early American Weathervanes

For centuries, weathervanes have prominently ornamented American town and country architecture. Carving these jaunty, stylized, wind-pointing horses, fish, birds and other animals and objects, at once decorative and utilitarian, is one of America's oldest and most familiar folk arts. With the patterns and instructions in this book, plus a few simple tools and materials, you will find it surprisingly easy to carve your own weathervanes in traditional styles. These sixteen projects are all replicas of authentic weathervane designs of the eighteenth, nineteenth and early twentieth centuries.

The only component that you cannot easily construct yourself is an old-fashioned standard, with balls and compass points (see Figure 1). Check antique dealers if you want one of these. Many of the great number manufactured are still around. But such an elaborate mount is not really necessary. I have a simple fish vane mounted on a brass rod in front of my home. Plain rods like this are perfectly suitable and may be obtained from local hardware stores. In any case, purchase a mount of suitable size. A larger vane will require a proportionately longer rod.

The following instructions apply generally to all the vanes in this book. Specific modifications may also apply to certain projects, so before doing anything, read through these instructions, as well as any specific instructions printed on the plate for the project of your choice.

Decide upon the size of your weathervane. If you want to make your vane the same size as the pattern for it in the center section of this book (make sure you buy a rod of suitable size), the pattern may be used as an exact-size template. Beginners will find this an easy way to carve their first weathervane. To use the patterns as templates, remove the staples from the book. Separate the pages with the patterns and spread them flat. Carefully cut out the pattern for the project of your choice (the

project on Plate 1, "Dexter," has an additional pattern for visual reference only, not to be used as a template), and save the information and instructions printed on the pattern pages. If you plan on reusing the templates, you can make them last longer by gluing them to cardboard. For real durability, glue them to wood; any #1 grade of exterior plywood about 3⁄16″ thick will do. After gluing, carefully recut the patterns and use varnish to seal the edges.

You can make larger or smaller weathervanes by enlarging or reducing the patterns. There are many ways of doing this. The grid method, using graph paper, is one of the best and easiest. If you are unfamiliar with this method, you may wish to use *The Artist's and Craftsman's Guide to Reducing, Enlarging and Transferring Designs* by Rita Weiss (Dover 24142-4), which comes with a supply of special graph paper.

Only after you have determined the size of your weathervane should you obtain materials. For larger vanes, use heavier rods and thicker wood. Remember that the diameter of the rod will determine that of the hole you drill into the wood. The size of the hole will in turn determine the thickness of the wood. For strength use stock sufficiently thick to allow plenty of wood to remain in the margins between the hole and the sides of the board. This is a vulnerable area and you can strengthen this hole further by inserting into it a length of brass tubing. If you do this, be sure, in order for the resulting hole to accommodate the supporting rod, that you drill a slightly larger hole in the wood and that the wood is thick enough to allow for the larger hole.

When you are certain of all these things, you are ready to consider purchasing the wood. The two basic kinds of wood are the hardwoods and the softwoods. Softwoods include such woods as white pine, white cedar, spruce and western red cedar. Among the hardwoods are ash, black walnut, mahogany, oak and maple. They are heavier than softwoods and generally more difficult to carve. I've used basswood for several of the projects in this book (see the color photographs on the covers). Basswood is classed as a hardwood, but it is close-grained and easily carved. I would call it a "soft hardwood." By all means experiment with various kinds of wood. Learning the different working qualities of wood can be a lifelong study in itself. For those who wish to learn more, a number of publications are available on this interesting subject.

Whichever wood you choose for your weathervane, it is important that it be well seasoned. Air-dried is best but regular kiln-dried stock obtained from lumberyards is suitable. Avoid "green" or unseasoned wood: it will warp and shrink and will not hold paint well.

When selecting boards, also be sure that the grain is such that it will run along the length of the shape to be carved out. Some patterns, particularly if you enlarge them, will require you to edge-join a number of boards to achieve the proper dimensions. When you do this, always alternate the direction of the growth rings visible on the ends of the boards (see Fig. 2). This will prevent warping in the finished piece. Also check

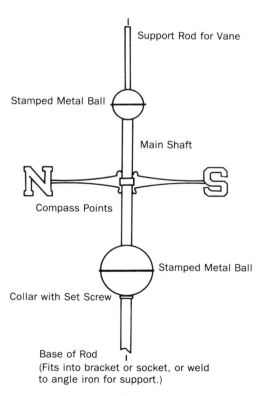

Support Rod for Vane

Stamped Metal Ball

Main Shaft

N   S

Compass Points

Stamped Metal Ball

Collar with Set Screw

Base of Rod
(Fits into bracket or socket, or weld to angle iron for support.)

FIG. 1

Rings Down   Rings Up   Rings Down

FIG. 2

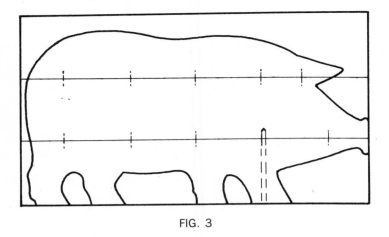

FIG. 3

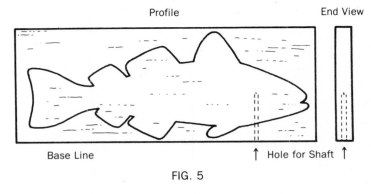

Profile   End View

Base Line   ↑ Hole for Shaft ↑

FIG. 5

all boards to be sure that they are of equal thickness. For small vanes, edge-joining can be done with a good-quality water-proof glue. For larger vanes, it may be necessary to use dowel pins and glue. Fig. 3 shows an edge-joined board for a large pig vane, indicating the position of the dowel pins and of the hole for the mount. To drill properly aligned holes for the dowel pins, you will need to use a doweling jig or similar device. These are widely available from woodworking supply houses. Unless you plan to make many large vanes, it will be quicker and less expensive to have a mill or cabinet shop provide you with the glued-up stock.

Another point must be considered. Certain vanes, particularly those with figures of long-legged animals, must be made of at least two edge-joined pieces with the grain of each running perpendicular (at a 90° angle) to that of the other. In Fig. 4, note that the grain of the bottom piece runs along the legs of the horse to give them strength. This bottom piece might itself have to be constructed of two or more edge-joined boards, depending on the size of the vane and the stock available at your local lumber supplier.

←—Grain—→

Doweled and Glued Joint

Grain →
← Grain

FIG. 4

Once you have obtained the appropriate wood, with any separate pieces properly edge-joined where necessary and with the grain running in the right direction, you are ready to create the shape. First, trace the pattern onto the wood. Next, drill the hole for the shaft of the mount. Draw a line across the base of the board where the hole is to be drilled, measure and mark the halfway point on this line, and drill at this point. Be careful here. It is extremely important for the hole to be at an angle of exactly 90° to the base of the board (which itself should be perfectly flat and regular), not just when viewed from the side but also when viewed from the end (see Fig. 5). Here is where a doweling jig really comes in handy. I must tell you, though, that with practice (use scrap!) you should be able to drill a reasonably straight hole without a jig. However you accomplish this, it pays to take pains at this point. If the hole is not correctly aligned, the vane will not pivot freely on its mount and will be useless as an indicator of wind direction.

After you have drilled the hole, saw out the shape of the pattern. Don't forget to follow any specific instructions that appear on the pattern-plate for your project. As a guide to even carving, draw a pencil line all around the half-thickness of the wood. You will then have a reference point to enable you to make symmetrical reductions in the thickness of fins, wings, etc. Use chisels to pare away excess wood from these areas. Round out the remaining edges of the sawn-out vane, and sand smooth. At this point any details such as eyes, ears, feathers or fins and finely textured areas may be carved in and sanded smooth. Follow any specific instructions regarding the addition of extra features, if applicable. When you have gained some experience in carving weathervanes, you may wish to experiment by adding bits of sheet metal to represent various features—antlers, fins, etc.—as was the practice with many homemade vanes in the old days. Let your imagination go— you may be surprised at the results!

All that remains is to consider whether you want to finish your vane or leave it unfinished. Wooden weathervanes were usually painted, but if you want the vane to acquire a weather-worn appearance very rapidly, just mount it and let the weather do its work. In time the elements will turn most woods a soft gray. If you prefer some color but still enjoy that weathered look, just paint directly on the bare wood using oil-based paints.

To really protect the wood, apply two coats of primer. Remember to use oil paint if you intend to apply oil primer. Latex primer is suitable for either oil or acrylic paint. Tube acrylics can be used for some of the brighter colors.